AF614944

GREAT SPORTS RIVALRIES

Jamie Fickett

THE LOS ANGELES LAKERS

A Stingray Book

Teaching Tips for Caregivers and Teachers:

This Hi-Lo book features high-interest subject matter that will appeal to all readers in intermediate and middle school grades. It may be enjoyed by students reading at or above grade level as well as by those who are looking for age-appropriate themes matched with a less challenging reading level. Hi-Lo books are ideal for ELL readers, too.

Each book appeals to a striving reader's age and maturity level. Opportunities are provided for students to read words they already know while encountering a limited number of new, high-interest vocabulary words. With these supports in place, students will read more fluently while increasing reading comprehension. Use the following suggestions to help students grow as readers.

- Encourage the student to read independently at home.
- Encourage the student to practice reading aloud.
- Encourage activities that require reading.
- Establish a regular reading time.
- Have the student write questions about what they read.

Teaching Tips for Teachers:

Before Reading

- Ask, "What do I know about this topic?"
- Ask, "What do I want to learn about this topic?"

During Reading

- Ask, "What is the author trying to teach me?"
- Ask, "How is this like something I already know?"

After Reading

- Discuss how the text features (headings, index, etc.) help with understanding the topic.
- Ask, "What interesting or fun fact did you learn?"

TABLE OF CONTENTS

COMPETITORS ON THE COURT

Some of the greatest basketball players of all time have played for the Boston Celtics and the Los Angeles Lakers. Matchups are always intense and action-packed.

But these NBA (National Basketball Association) teams don't like each other very much. Their fierce **rivalry** is legendary.

The teams have met in at least 298 regular-season games. Of these games, the Celtics won 165, and the Lakers won 133.

FUN FACT

Boston, Massachusetts, is on the East Coast of the United States. Los Angeles, California, is on the West Coast.

bibigo
LAKERS
0
BOSTON
36

1940s and 1950s: THE RIVALRY BEGINS

From 1947 to 1960, the Lakers were based in Minneapolis, Minnesota. Through much of the 1950s, the Lakers were a **dynasty**. They dominated most other teams.

But the Celtics could beat them. They first played the Lakers in 1948. The Celtics won 77 to 55.

In the 1959 NBA Finals, the Celtics swept the Lakers 4 games to 0. It was the first Finals loss for the Lakers.

FUN FACT

In 1960, the Minneapolis Lakers became the Los Angeles Lakers.

1960s: HEAD-TO-HEAD

Throughout the 1960s, the Lakers and the Celtics were the strongest teams in the NBA.

The Celtics played in the NBA Finals every year of the decade. They lost only once.

In six of those Finals, they played against the Lakers.

In 1968, star **center** Wilt Chamberlain joined the Lakers. He had a personal rivalry with Celtics center Bill Russell.

FUN FACT

Bill Russell won 11 NBA Championships.

Bill Russell

1979: A RIVALRY RETURNS

Larry Bird

Magic Johnson

After a ten-year gap, the rivalry started up again in the 1979 season.

That year, the Lakers **drafted** Magic Johnson. The Celtics drafted Larry Bird. The two powerhouses had played each other in college. Their famous rivalry continued in the NBA.

That season, Bird won NBA Rookie of the Year. But Magic was the Finals MVP. The Lakers won the NBA Championship.

FUN FACT

Bird kept track of how many points Magic scored in his games. Magic paid attention to all the Celtics games.

1982: LAKERS ON TOP

It was the final game of the 1982 Eastern Conference Finals. The Celtics were playing for a chance to meet the Lakers in the NBA Finals. Celtics fans started to chant, "Beat L.A.!"

But the Celtics lost to the Philadelphia 76ers.

The Lakers were at the top of their game with their new head coach Pat Riley. They won the 1982 Championship over the 76ers.

FUN FACT

Pat Riley played both basketball and football as a student at the University of Kentucky.

Pat Riley

1980s: FIGHTS IN THE FINALS

Kevin McHale

Kareem Abdul-Jabbar

FUN FACT

Lakers legend Kareem Abdul-Jabbar is the second-highest scoring player in NBA history. Only LeBron James has scored more points.

The rivals met in the 1984 NBA Finals. They were tied after the first two games. Game 3 was a blowout with a Celtics win 137 to 104.

In game 4, a **brawl** broke out when Celtics player Kevin McHale **clotheslined** Lakers forward Kurt Rambis. The Celtics were crowned 1984 Champions.

The next year, the Lakers were back on top. They defeated the Celtics in six games to win the 1985 NBA Finals.

The Lakers won the Championship again in 1987. They won four games in the Finals, and the Celtics won two.

2000s: CELTICS RISE

The Celtics had losing records for much of the 1990s. But in the mid-2000s, they built a winning team with strong players like **guard** Ray Allen and **forwards** Paul Pierce and Kevin Garnett.

The Celtics met the Lakers in the 2008 NBA Finals. Los Angeles had standout center Pau Gasol and star guard Kobe Bryant.

Boston won the Championship with a score of 131 to 92 in the last game.

FUN FACT

Kobe Bryant was drafted into the NBA straight out of high school.

Kobe Bryant

2010: LAKERS COMEBACK

The rivals faced off again in the 2010 NBA Finals.

Boston kept their winning trio of Pierce, Garnett, and Allen. Los Angeles still had power duo Bryant and Gasol.

It all came down to game 7. The Lakers were behind. Then, in the fourth quarter, they came back to beat the Celtics 83 to 79 and win the Championship.

FUN FACT

The Lakers and the Celtics are tied for most NBA Championships. They have both won the title 17 times.

THE RIVALRY CONTINUES

Today's star players continue the **epic** rivalry between the Boston Celtics and the Los Angeles Lakers.

Boston forwards Jayson Tatum and Jaylen Brown play against Los Angeles center Anthony Davis.

Who will win the next battle between these two great teams?

FUN FACT

The Celtics beat the Lakers 126 to 115 on Christmas Day 2023. Centers Kristaps Porzingis and Anthony Davis both got a double-double.

GLOSSARY

brawl (brawl): a rough or noisy fight

center (SEN-tur): a player whose job is to score on close shots and rebounds, to block opponents' shots, and to rebound their misses; often the tallest player on the team

clotheslined (KLOZH-lined): knocked a player down by catching him by the neck with an outstretched arm

drafted (DRAF-tid): selected to play on a team

dynasty (DYE-nuh-stee): a team that dominates their sport for a long time

epic (EP-ik): amazing or impressive

forwards (FOR-wurdz): players whose job is to attack and score goals

guard (gahrd): a player who works in the backcourt to initiate plays

rivalry (RYE-vuhl-ree): a longstanding, competitive, up-and-down relationship between two teams

INDEX

AFTER READING QUESTIONS

1. Which team has won more against the other in regular-season games?
2. What players joined the Celtics in the 2000s?
3. What caused a brawl to break out at the 1984 NBA Finals?
4. Describe the relationship between Magic Johnson and Larry Bird.
5. Which team did Kobe Bryant play for in the 2010 NBA Finals?

ABOUT THE AUTHOR

Jamie Fickett lives in Long Island, New York. He enjoys sports, especially baseball. He likes to go to Mets games to watch his favorite player, Pete Alonso, play. He also enjoys cooking his famous chili and watching Formula 1 racing.

Written by: Jamie Fickett
Design by: Kathy Walsh
Editor: Kim Thompson

Library of Congress PCN Data
The Boston Celtics vs. The Los Angeles Lakers
/Jamie Fickett
Great Sports Rivalries
ISBN 979-8-8873-5951-9 (hard cover)
ISBN 979-8-8873-5990-8 (paperback)
ISBN 979-8-8904-2049-7 (EPUB)
ISBN 979-8-8904-2108-1 (eBook)
Library of Congress Control Number: 2023912511

Printed in the United States of America.

Photographs/Shutterstock/Newscom: Cover: Marty Jean-Louis, Jim Ruymen; p 5, 6, 9, 10, 13, 14, 17, 18, 21: Fotokita; p 5: Burt Harris; p 6: Rose Palmisano; p 9: @Wiki; p 10: John McDonough/ Icon SMI; p 13: Jeff Widener / UPI Photo Service/ Newscom p 14: Steve Lipofsky; p 17: Phil McCarten; p 18: Rose Palmisano; p 21: Jevone Moore

Seahorse Publishing Company
www.seahorsepub.com

Copyright © 2025 **SEAHORSE PUBLISHING COMPANY**

All rights reserved. No part of this publication may be reproduced, stored in a retrieval system or be transmitted in any form or by any means, electronic, mechanical, photocopying, recording, or otherwise, without the prior written permission of Seahorse Publishing Company.

Published in the United States
Seahorse Publishing
PO Box 771325
Coral Springs, FL 33077